# Around Matlock

## IN OLD PHOTOGRAPHS

THE ASCENDING DOUCHE.
"Now Sir, please to take a seat here."

A satirical print.

# Around Matlock

## IN OLD PHOTOGRAPHS

### Collected by DAVID A. BARTON

In collaboration with
Derbyshire County Council

Alan Sutton Publishing Limited
Phoenix Mill · Far Thrupp
Stroud · Gloucestershire

DERBYSHIRE
County Council

First published 1993

Copyright © David A. Barton, 1993

British Library Cataloguing in Publication Data

Barton, David
Around Matlock in Old Photographs
I. Title
942.513

ISBN 0-7509-0502-6

Typeset in 9/10 Sabon.
Typesetting and origination by
Alan Sutton Publishing Limited.
Printed in Great Britain by
Redwood Books, Trowbridge.

# Contents

Crown Square and cable tramway, Matlock. The clock above the bus shelter was presented to the town by Robert Wildgoose in 1899. This postcard is postmarked 1921.

# Introduction

*Matlock must be allowed to possess superior advantages to the generality of watering places. It has gaiety without dissipation, activity without noise and facility of communication with other parts of the country undisturbed by the bustle of a public road . . .*

These glowing words, written in 1802 by George Lipscomb, a geologist and spa enthusiast, refer to Matlock Bath, then in its heyday as a spa. Matlock Bath's dramatic scenery had been admired by generations of tourists. It was visited by Daniel Defoe, Celia Fiennes and Samuel Johnson in the eighteenth century, and in the nineteenth century it was much admired by Lord Byron and John Ruskin. Before 1698 Matlock Bath consisted of a few scattered houses, but soon the warm springs began to attract attention for their medicinal properties and the first bath was built. Second and third baths were added later, together with attached hotel accommodation. By 1830 these hotels and innumerable lodging houses could cater for more than four hundred people. Later on, however, as seaside resorts became fashionable, the popularity of inland spas declined. The local historian, Bryan, writing in 1903, attributes Matlock Bath's decline in popularity to the coming of the railway in 1849, which brought in the day-trippers in their thousands. Perhaps a more important factor lay in its geographical situation, which made expansion almost impossible. When the Matlock area expanded further, as it did in the second half of the nineteenth century, it was on the other side of the river in the area that is now Matlock Bank.

Before the end of the nineteenth century Matlock was merely a collection of nucleated settlements, with a feeling of separateness that still survives today. The two main settlements were Matlock Bath and Matlock Bank. This book covers the Matlock area, together with the outlying areas of Darley Dale, Cromford, Bonsall and Tansley.

The second half of the nineteenth century saw the development of Matlock Bank as a hydropathic area. Hydropathy, the practice of treating disease by the application of water, had been known since Greek and Roman times but was revived in England in the nineteenth century, largely through the introduction of ideas from the Continent. John Smedley (1803–74), a local hosiery manufacturer, after enduring a cure at Ben Rhydding in Yorkshire, decided to establish his own hydro. It was opened in 1853 and, with its subsequent enlargements, has dominated the Matlock skyline ever since. Other hydros were built, often by ex-employees of Smedley and with his help, some catering for the wealthy and others for the less well-off. In addition to the water treatment the hydros provided a regime very like that of the modern health farm: alcohol was banned, tobacco prohibited and spices used not at all. In the later, more permissive, days, however, some of these restrictions were relaxed somewhat: certainly after 1900 enormous meals seem to have been served at festive times. Many of the hydros were used by the services during both world wars, but after 1945 hydropathy gradually became less fashionable and they were converted for other purposes. Several became part of the new teacher training college that was set up at Matlock after the Second World War. Smedley's Hydro continued until in 1955 when, sadly dilapidated, it was bought by the Derbyshire County Council. Now renovated and refurbished, it is the county council offices.

Darley Dale, like Matlock a collection of disjointed settlements, lies along the A6 between Matlock and Bakewell. Local industries included quarrying (the stone from Stancliffe quarries was sent to all parts of the country, some being used in Trafalgar Square) and lead mining (Mill Close Mine, which closed as a mine in 1939, was the biggest in the country), and several plant nurseries were established there. The railway, before the closure of the line to Manchester in the 1960s, employed many local people. A large number of the amenities enjoyed in Darley today were started by Sir Joseph Whitworth (1803–87) and his wife, who settled in Darley in 1871.

Down the A6 to the south, past Matlock Bath, lies Cromford, the industrial village where, in 1772, Sir Richard Arkwright (1732–92) established the first cotton mill to be worked by water power. Arkwright was responsible for most of the buildings in this industrial village, including the Greyhound inn and the church. His own house, Willersley Castle, overlooks the village.

Overshadowed by Cromford, and sometimes overlooked, Bonsall is an old lead-mining village, with its church standing high up. Along the A615 in the direction of Alfreton is the village of Tansley, with its tiny Victorian church. In the distance may be seen John Smedley's residence, Riber Castle, now a fauna reserve.

The religious atmosphere of the area has always been strongly nonconformist and predominantly Methodist. Matlock had three principal Methodist chapels: the Wesleyan and Primitive Methodist chapels on Bank Road, and the United Methodist chapel on Imperial Road. Of these only the Wesleyan chapel is still in use for religious purposes. It has been said that Methodism was born in song. Certainly one result of the Methodist influence on Matlock has been the creation of a choral tradition, formerly chapel-based, which continues to this day. The present Matlock Choir is descended from the Primitive Methodist Prize Choir, which, under the baton of Lubin Wildgoose, achieved many successes. The tradition lives on in the person of the present conductor, Mrs Gloria Hollingworth, the granddaughter of Lubin Wildgoose. Brass bands, too, have always been a feature of Matlock. Here the seminal figure was Fred Slater (1896–1982). Under his tutelage many locals have become proficient on brass instruments, and this is carried on by his son Murray. Other features of Matlock include amateur dramatics, poultry shows, which were once strongly supported by fanciers but are now declining in popularity, and still retaining its attraction is the procession of illuminated boats at Matlock Bath, which, accompanied by firework displays and band concerts, has long been part of the autumn scene in Matlock.

The story of photography begins in 1841 when William Henry Fox Talbot patented his Calotype, the forerunner of the modern photograph. By 1861, 2,534 professional photographers were at work. Surviving photographs from that era include those taken by Roger Fenton in the Crimean War and the even more dramatic pictures taken by Matthew Brady in the American Civil War. The wet collodion process, as used then, demanded both dexterity and an uncanny degree of chemical expertise on the part of the photographer. It also required much equipment – Brady travelled with a horse-drawn mobile darkroom – and it was not until the introduction of roll film in the 1890s and the Box Brownie in 1900 that photography became easy and relatively cheap. With the introduction of faster film, more informal and spontaneous pictures became possible and the snapshot era began.

The compiler of a book of this type is necessarily constrained by the amount and quality of material at his disposal. There are no photographs here from the early period; the majority are taken from postcards, which first appeared on the British scene in 1894 and became very popular with holiday-makers. Without the help of friends in the Matlock area who lent me photographs, particularly Glyn Waite and Ken Smith, this book could not have been put together.

David A. Barton

8

# SECTION ONE

# Matlock and the Hydros

Matlock Bridge and Bank. Smedley's Hydro is at the top left of this postcard, which was probably produced at around the turn of the century. In the middle is Bank Road, the route of the cable tramway. The gradient of this road is very severe, rising 300 ft in half a mile.

Crown Square, *c*. 1914. The shops on the right were demolished in the mid-1920s.

Crown Square, *c*. 1925. The bus (left) belongs to William Furniss, a local bus and carriage proprietor.

Dale Road, looking south. Now the A6 and blighted by traffic, this was once the main shopping street of Matlock. The former Queen's Head is on the right. This view probably dates to sometime before the First World War.

Farther along Dale Road. The Old English Hotel is on the left and Pilkington's chemist is on the right. Two horse-drawn sightseeing vehicles occupy the greater part of the road.

Dale Road, looking north. The Old English Hotel is on the right in this unusually quiet road.

Matlock Bridge. The bridge was built in medieval times and widened in 1904. This postcard, printed after 1904, shows the Matlock skyline with Smedley's Hydro in a prominent position (top left).

Job Smith. Job was a man of many parts who lived until just before the First World War. He was the owner of Malvern House Hydro on Smedley Street and the first county councillor for the Matlock district, to name just one of the several offices he held. His chief claim to fame locally was for his efforts to bring a cable tramway to Matlock, which he achieved in 1893.

The official opening of Matlock cable tramway, 1893. The tramway was opened on 28 March of this year and finally closed on 23 September 1927. Job Smith (top deck, third from right) and other local worthies are pictured just before the ceremony.

A Matlock cable tramcar, standing at the top of Rutland Street, 1904. The trams were pulled up Matlock Bank by a continuously moving cable, which ran in a steel drum under the road. Their top speed was 5 miles per hour. This picture was taken by the noted local photographer W.N. Statham, whose studio was on Dale Road.

The interior of a Matlock cable tramcar, before 1917. This picture was taken on the traverser in the tram shed, which can still be seen at the top of Rutland Street. Although the seating may appear uncomfortable, it was not untypical of tramcars. I recall riding in trams of a similar type in Birmingham in the 1930s and 1940s. The tramway in Matlock was never profitable and by 1917 was losing £1,000 a year. It was closed in 1927. This picture also was taken by W.N. Statham.

John Wildgoose in the doorway of his flower and fruit shop on Smedley Street.

Mr William Evans and his son Walter outside Evans & Son, Dale Road. This long-established jewellers is still on Dale Road. The picture dates from the early years of this century.

Stanley Fearn in front of Stanley Fearn & Son, Bakewell Road, *c.* 1920s.

Stanley Fearn & Son, Bakewell Road, 1954.

Michael Wright and a delivery van belonging to M. Wright & Sons, Smedley Street. Michael, locally known as 'Tinker', is described in a directory as a 'hydropathic bath and patent ascending douche manufacturer, general tin, iron, copper, zinc-sheet worker and general ironmonger'. The firm, which still flourishes, was founded in 1870 and owed much to the inventiveness of Mr Wright, who patented his ascending douche (see p. 2). His hollow tin-ware chest-warmers were highly thought of and his firm had an extensive postal trade in hydropathic goods.

Snowfalls in Matlock. The winter of 1946/7 was bad all over the country, but in Matlock it was especially hard. This picture shows the depth of snow and an intrepid motorist.

Snowfalls in Wellington Street, winter 1946/7. The Duke of Wellington (right) seems to be cut off.

Floods in Bakewell Road, 1907. Until the recent defences were built, Matlock was often affected by heavy winter floods, notably in 1901 and 1931.

Floods, viewed from the bottom of the Dimple, December 1965. Stanley Fearn's shop is on the far side of the road (centre).

John Smedley (1803–74). Smedley may be said to have been the man who put Matlock on the map. A textile manufacturer at Lea Mills near Matlock, he was cured of a serious illness by treatment at Ben Rhydding, a hydropathic establishment near Ilkley in Yorkshire. He returned to Matlock and went into partnership with Ralph Davis in an establishment on Matlock Bank, then relatively unpopulated. In 1853 he took over the practice and began to build his own hydro, and in 1867 he and his wife treated two thousand patients. The Smedley cure was of a milder nature than some in that the water used was tepid rather than icy cold. By the turn of the century there were over twenty hydros in Matlock as many ex-employees of Smedley's Hydro set up their own establishments. This photograph of Smedley is one of the very few that exist.

Riber Castle, private residence of John Smedley. The castle was built by Smedley in 1862 at a cost of £60,000. After his death it became a preparatory school and was later used as a food store. It is now a fauna reserve.

Smedley's Hydro.

Smedley's Hydro. In the distance are the Winter Garden and the spire of the United Methodist Free church, built by Smedley but converted to a dynamo house after his death.

The drawing-room, Smedley's Hydro.

The Winter Garden, Smedley's Hydro.

Ron Farrell's Band, Smedley's Hydro, late 1940s. Left to right: Ron Farrell, Derek Lane, Harry Boden, Ben Wood, Joe Spencer.

Rockside Hydro. This was opened by Charles Rowland in 1862. The picture, taken from stationery, shows the original building.

Rockside Hydro. The building was substantially altered by Parker and Unwin in 1903–6.

The interior of Rockside Hydro.

The ballroom, Rockside Hydro.

Rockside Hydro as a training college. After service as an RAF psychiatric hospital during the Second World War, Rockside became part of the new Matlock Training College, which at first catered only for girls. These pictures are from a brochure of the early 1950s.

Chesterfield House Hydro. Built in 1861 in extensive grounds on the Chesterfield Road, this hydro was some distance from the centre of Matlock. It closed in 1927 and was taken over by the Presentation Convent, by which it is still owned. This postcard is postmarked 1907.

Bank House Hydro. This later became Wyvern House Hydro and then the Ernest Bailey Grammar School. Part of the building is now used as the County Record Office.

Matlock House Hydro. This was opened in 1863 by a Mr Lee of Manchester.

Lilybank Hydro. This was opened in 1890 by George Barton as Dalefield, but the name was changed to Lilybank in 1906. It ceased to be a hydro in the 1950s and was bought by the Presentation Convent as a school.

Jeff's Poplar Hydro. Opened in 1857 with over two hundred beds, the name was later changed to Chatsworth Hydro. It was used as a hospital in both world wars and then became part of Matlock Training College. This postcard is postmarked 1903.

Residents relaxing in the grounds of Jeff's Poplar Hydro.

Oldham House Hydro. This hydro was opened in 1890. At the turn of the century it was amalgamated with Prospect Place, which had been opened in 1859 by Thomas Davis. During the Second World War the hydro was used by the RAF as a hospital. It later became part of Matlock Training College. This postcard is postmarked 1929.

The dining-room, Oldham House Hydro.

This is a mystery picture since no one seems to have any knowledge of Tilley's Hydro.

The Lindens old people's home, formerly a Nalgo convalescent home. This was a guest-house in the nineteenth century, and Dante Gabriel Rossetti and Elizabeth Siddall, later his wife, stayed there in 1857.

ROCK & Cᵒ 0202
LONDON.

Costume of the Establishᵗ.
Doing Penance in the Wet Sheet

A satirical print.

A satirical print.

Rose Cottage Hydro.

The Dimple. Before the building of the A6 this was the beginning of the Matlock to Bakewell Road.

Bank Road.

Matlock from Matlock Bank. Smedley's Hydro is on the left.

Soldiers on Smedley Street. During the Second World War Smedley's Hydro was used for military intelligence courses. Among the well-known people attending these courses were Evelyn Waugh, Anthony Powell and Dirk Bogarde.

Warrant officers, staff sergeants and sergeants at Smedley's Hydro when it was the Intelligence Training Centre, November 1941. Front row, fourth from left is Col. Benfield DSO MC.

Members of a training course at Smedley's Hydro, 1943.

Officers at Smedley's Hydro, 27 March 1944. Front row, left to right: Capt. P.W. Skipper, Capt. W.F. Lawrence, Maj. W. Forsyth, Maj. St J.P. Draper, Brig. W.J. Jervois MC (Commandant), Maj. R.C. Moles, Maj. Newcombe, Maj. K.M.J. Dewar, Maj. A.R.M. Greenly. Middle row: Capt. I.E.W. Besley, Maj. H.T. Snean, Maj. K.I. Topliss, Maj. D.P.J. Lloyd, Maj. R.J.T. Pollock, Capt. Sir P. Norton Griffiths Bt, Maj. N.H.L. Chesshyre, Maj. R.M. Firth. Back row: Maj. K.N.H. Thomson, Maj. J. Mark, Maj. A.R. Whately-Smith, Capt. A.C. Bridge, Capt. E.P. Wallis Jones, Capt. K.L. Dod.

Victory Ball at Smedley's Hydro, Thursday 10 May 1945.

Claremont. Now an old people's home, this was the home of Charles Rowland, who opened Rockside Hydro in 1862.

Smedley's Memorial Hydropathic Hospital. This was built by Mrs Smedley as a memorial to her husband. It was opened in 1882 and is now a youth hostel.

St Giles' church, the old parish church. Alterations were made in 1859 and 1871 by Benjamin Wilson of Derby, and a chancel was added in 1898 by P.H. Currey.

The interior of All Saints' church, Matlock Bank. This church was built in 1883/4 and the architects were T.H. and F. Healey.

Congregational church, Chesterfield Road, Matlock Bank. This church was opened in 1866 and the architect was W. Hull of Northampton. It has now been demolished.

The interior of the Congregational church, Chesterfield Road, Matlock Bank.

# MATLOCK
# WESLEYAN METHODIST CIRCUIT.

**Ministers.**
Rev. WILLIAM TALBOT, Matlock Bridge.
Rev. E. THEO. CARRIER, Matlock Bath.
Rev. THOMAS SHELDON, Cromford.

**Circuit Stewards.**
Mr. HENRY MARSDEN, Matlock Bank.

### ➤✳WESLEYAN✳CHAPEL,✳MATLOCK✳BRIDGE✳✳◀

The freehold site on which the above Chapel is being built is 110 feet in length, and 79 feet in breadth; and the Chapel, with its spire 110 feet in height, will be 69 feet in length and 43 feet in breadth, and will seat 340 adults on the ground floor and 116 in the gallery.

The cost of the present effort, including site and school-room underneath, is £2,330. Towards this amount we have in subscriptions paid and promised, £872; we expect to realise by the sale of the Old Chapel about £400; the Committee of the Extension Fund for Methodism have promised a grant of £80; and the Chapel Committee a grant of £40, with a loan of £100 without interest repayable in ten years. It is hoped also that £200 may be raised at the Foundation Stone and Opening Services, and £150 by a Bazaar. This will leave about £350 still to be raised. The Matlock Bridge friends earnestly ask for Subscriptions from all the places in the Circuit.

An elaborate preaching plan for the Matlock Wesleyan Methodist Circuit. It was issued for the opening of the new Wesleyan chapel in 1882. The architect was C.O. Ellison of Liverpool, who took advantage of the sloping site. Although the drawing depicts a spire, it was not until more than twenty years later that this feature was added.

NEW PORCH
— and —
— TOWER —
WESLEYAN CHURCH
MATLOCK BRIDGE

Matlock Wesleyan chapel. The tower and porch were finally added in 1904. The architect was Horace G. Bradley of Birmingham. This drawing is taken from the report of the Wesleyan Chapel Building Committee.

Matlock.

Fox Memorial, Starkh[...]

Rev. Jas. Burton.

Matlock Moor

Hackney.

A postcard for the Matlock Primitive Methodist Circuit. This was issued between 1901 and 1907, when James Burton was the superintendent minister. Primitive Methodism was strong in Matlock, and the Bank Road chapel (top left) was very well attended, its congregation swelled by visitors staying at nearby Smedley's Hydro.

# SECTION TWO

# Matlock Bath

North Parade, Matlock Bath.

South Parade, Matlock Bath. This card possibly dates from before the First World War.

North Parade, Matlock Bath. The date of this view is similar to that of the previous picture.

Royal Hotel, Matlock Bath. This hotel was built in 1878 on the site of the old bath and destroyed by fire in 1927.

Fairview Terrace, Matlock Bath. The growing popularity of the bicycle in the 1890s opened Matlock up to the more intrepid cyclist.

Jubilee Bridge, Matlock Bath, opened in June 1887. This postcard is postmarked 1910.

Holy Trinity Church, Matlock Bath. This church, designed by Weightman and Hadfield, was built in 1842. Alterations were made in 1873/4 by T.E. Streatfield.

St John's chapel of ease, Matlock Bath. This chapel was built by Sir Guy Dawber in 1897.

The interior of St John's chapel of ease, Matlock Bath, showing the Stations of the Cross.

Lady Glenorchy's chapel, Matlock Bath. This chapel was opened in 1785 and demolished in 1951 when the road was widened.

River Derwent, Matlock Bath. The Wesleyan Methodist chapel (centre) was opened in 1865 and was designed by Henry Fuller of Manchester. This postcard was sent between 1910 and 1935.

Matlock Bath Wesleyan chapel.
This print is from the Wesleyan
Chapel Building Committee
Report.

North Parade, Matlock Bath.

North Parade, Matlock Bath.

Temple Hotel, Matlock Bath, 1 March 1920. Left to right: Mr Charles Farmer, Miss F. Farmer, Sarah Harrison (in invalid chair).

The Grand Pavilion, Matlock Bath. This pavilion was built in 1910 and has been the venue for many activities over the years.

River Derwent, Matlock Bath. The illuminations have long been a feature of the late summer season. Saturday evenings usually include a brass band concert and end with a firework display.

Illuminated boats, Matlock Bath. There has for many years been a competition for the best illuminated boat. Originally candles were used. The two boats featured here were the winners in 1927 (top) and 1922 (bottom).

# SECTION THREE
# Cromford

The market-place, Cromford. Cromford was only a small village when Sir Richard Arkwright built his mill in 1771. The mill, driven by the water of the nearby Derwent, was the first of the many hundreds of mills later built all over England. Much of the building in Cromford was by Arkwright, including the Greyhound Hotel and a second mill, Masson Mill, built in 1783.

The market-place, Cromford, looking up Cromford Hill.

The market-place, Cromford, looking down Cromford Hill.

Derby Road, Cromford. This is the present A6 in quieter days, showing a brake with sightseers (left).

Cromford Bridge and church. This bridge dates from the fifteenth century. The church, which was completed in 1797, after Arkwright's death, was probably designed by Thomas Gardner of Uttoxeter. It was gothicized in 1858.

Cromford Canal. Opened in 1793, this canal, which was 14¾ miles long, formed a waterway between Cromford and the towns of East Derbyshire and Nottinghamshire.

A view of Cromford looking across the dam to Scarthin.

Willersley Castle, Cromford. Built for Arkwright by William Thomas of London in 1789/90, this building was Classical in conception but has Gothic features. The interior was destroyed by fire in 1791 and redesigned by Thomas Gardner of Uttoxeter. It is now a Methodist holiday and conference centre.

The dining-room, Willersley Castle, Cromford, possibly 1940s.

Castletop Farm, Cromford. Alison Uttley (1884–1976), the author of many children's books, was born and spent her early life here.

# SECTION FOUR

# Bonsall and Via Gellia

Clatterway, Bonsall, seen from the higher part of the village. Bonsall was a centre for framework knitting in the eighteenth and nineteenth centuries.

The Pig of Lead, Bonsall, 1930s.

The Pig of Lead, Bonsall. The date of this view is earlier than that of the previous picture.

St James's parish church, Bonsall. This church was restored by Ewan Christian in 1862/3.

The interior of St James's church, Bonsall.

Keeper's House, Via Gellia. This is usually known as Tufa Cottage.

A choir outing on Via Gellia in a waggonette.

The Pig of Lead, Via Gellia, Matlock Bath.

Via Gellia. Despite its Latin name this road has no Roman connections. It was built in the eighteenth century by the Gell family to give access to their quarries at Hopton.

Rider Point, Via Gellia, near Bonsall.

Via Gellia from Middleton. The cottage is Mountain Cottage, where D.H. Lawrence and his wife, Frieda, lived for the greater part of 1918.

# Darley Dale

Darley Dale from Oaker Hill. Oaker Hill is mentioned in Wordsworth's poem:

'Tis said that to the brow of yon fair hill
Two brothers clomb, and turning face from face,
Nor one look more exchanging, grief to still,
Or feed, each planted on that lofty place
A chosen tree; . . .

The Darley Dale area was largely occupied by quarrying, lead mining and plant nurseries. Before the Beeching cuts, which closed the railway line to Manchester, many men worked on the railway.

A house on Bent Lane, Darley Hillside, *c.* 1914. The house is now called Dunelm.

Elm Tree Cottage, Bent Lane, Darley Hillside, *c.* 1917.

The township adjacent to Darley's medieval bridge, viewed from Darley Bridge.

The Grouse Inn, Darley Dale. This inn was built in 1824 by Heathcote Heathcote.

Sir Joseph Whitworth (1803–87). Sir Joseph was one of the great nineteenth-century mechanical engineers. He played a major part in the development of machine tools, in promoting absolute accuracy in measurement and in the standardization of machine parts. He bought Stancliffe Hall and its estate in 1856, taking up residence there in 1871.

The unveiling of the obelisk to Sir Joseph Whitworth in Whitworth Park, Darley Dale, 1894.

The Whitworth Institute and monument, Darley Dale. The Whitworth Institute, built in 1890, comprises a hotel, refreshment room and many other rooms, with provision for outdoor games.

Whitworth Park entrance, Darley Dale.

Boating on the ornamental lake at Whitworth Park. The lake has now been filled in.

Whitworth Hospital, Darley Dale. This hospital was opened in 1889 and paid for from Sir Joseph Whitworth's estate.

The junction between Chesterfield Road, Park Lane and Oddford Lane, Two Dales.

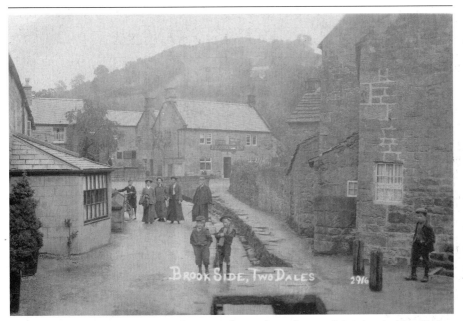

Brookside, Two Dales. The Plough Inn (right) is the only remaining inn in Two Dales. The two others, closed within the last thirty years, were The Nag's Head and The Blacksmith's Arms.

Losker Row, Two Dales. This industrial housing was built for millworkers. It has now been demolished.

The centre of the village of Two Dales, probably before the First World War. The man leaning against the wall is just outside The Blacksmith's Arms, now closed.

The centre of Two Dales village.

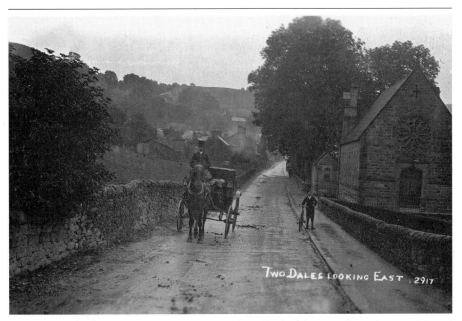

Chesterfield Road (now the B5057), Two Dales. The building on the right, now Hayes' bakery, was formerly a school and before that a mission room.

Brook Bottom, Two Dales.

The first anniversary of the Sunday School, Darley Hillside Methodist Chapel. A new chapel was built in 1912 by the then Primitive Methodists, replacing the old chapel at Northwood on Lumb Lane. The architect was D.M. Wildgoose. The choirmaster, S. Wardman, is in the front row.

The Two Dales Wesleyan Sunday School fife and drum band, outside the new chapel. In 1904 the Wesleyans in Darley Dale built a new chapel in Dale Road. It replaced the old chapel in Two Dales.

Bell-ringers from St Helen's church, Darley Dale, relaxing at Leek, Staffordshire, 1931. Left to right: Robert Allsopp, William Bagshawe, Eric Derbyshire, George Paulson, Edwin Blackwell, Herbert Taylor, Bernard Allsopp.

St Helen's church choir, Darley Dale, *c.* 1955. The Revd R.J. Stanford, the rector, is in the centre.

St Mary's church, Darley Dale. The gathering appears to be a church or chapel walk.

Three old employees of Thomas Smith, Two Dales.

Miss Fogg, standing in the garden of Springfield, Fogg's Hill, Darley Hillside.

Laburnum Cottage, Hallmoor Road, Darley Hillside.

# Tansley

Tansley village. This village sits astride the A615, which is the main Matlock to Alfreton Road. It had a hydro, run by William Mycock, a former employee of John Smedley's, as well as a variety of industries and nurseries.

Holy Trinity church, Tansley, designed by John Mason of Derby. This was built in 1839/40. It is a simple stone church in the Early English style. An aisle was added in 1869.

The Tansley Juvenile Society, Tansley, 1908. Judging by the banner there seem to be connections with the Oddfellows. Perhaps this was a junior branch.

The Marsh family outside the post office on the Knoll, Tansley, 1905.

F.H. Drabble & Sons Ltd., Tansley Wood Mills, Tansley.

Garton's and other mills, Lumsdale, Tansley.

Mr Dawes (and his wife or sister) outside Briddon's shop on The Cliff, close to Royal Oak, Tansley.

Clearing snow on Whitelea Lane, Tansley, 1947.

Horse and cart belonging to Vaughan Taylor of Spout Farm, Tansley, *c.* 1925.

A bull-nose Morris outside Spout Farm, Tansley, *c.* 1930.

Tansley post office, *c.* 1905.

A carnival procession, Tansley, *c.* 1930.

## SECTION SEVEN

# Earning a Living

Mill Close Mine, Darley Dale. This was once the largest lead mine in the country. It was flooded in 1939 and has not been mined since.

Mill Close Mine, Darley Dale, 1938. Left to right: Walter Boam, Ernest Moseley, Peter Marshall, John Henry Smith, Bill Marshall, Stan Else, Dick Slack.

Mill Close Mine, Darley Dale, 1930. Those present are: Bill Blackham, Arthur Vardy, Herbert Heathcote, Bert Webster, Les Flint, Thomas Webster, Chris Stone, Harry Taylor.

Mill Close Mine, Darley Dale, 1930. Back row, left to right: Harry Bowmer, Fred Flint, Wilf Spencer, Dick Bond, Edward Stevenson. Middle row: Stan Marshall, Owen Smith, George Kenworthy, Stan Maynes, Charlie Stewartson. Front row: E. Fisher, Harry Goodwin, Harold Boam.

Workers at Mill Close Mine, Darley Dale, 1930s.

Stancliffe Quarry, Darley Dale, showing the depth of rock that had been quarried.

Quarry workers, Darley Dale, *c.* 1921.

The blacksmith's shop, Stancliffe Quarry, Darley Dale.

Firth-Derihons (now Firth-Rixon) factory, 1942. This was built as a 'shadow' factory at the start of the Second World War. Those present include D. Pink, Rene Cartwright, Win Wardman, Eva Askew, Mr Prime, Carl Windley, Winnie Needham, Mrs Prime, Bob Hutchinson, H. Smedley and Jean Evans.

Members of Matlock Fire Brigade.

Harvesting in the Matlock area.

The Slack family, harvesting at Blakelow Farm, Bonsall Moor, 1927. Left to right: Olive, Tom, Eva, Samuel, Richard, Hannah, Arnold, Otto.

Arnold Slack in Homefield, Blakelow Farm, Bonsall Moor, late 1930s.

Samuel Slack, Blakelow Farm, Bonsall Moor, *c.* 1920

Eva Slack, Blakelow Farm, Bonsall Moor, late 1930s. The vehicle is a long-wheel-based Bedford lorry.

Mr Nightingale's traction engine and threshing machine, Tansley.

Vaughan Taylor (senior) ploughing, Tansley, 1930s.

A steamroller at the bottom of Holt Lane, Matlock, *c.* 1930.

John Barber, with young assistant, making rope at Rope Walk, off Green Lane, Tansley, 1932.

John Barber making rope, Tansley, 1932. These pictures were taken for the *Derbyshire Times*.

Outdoor and gardening staff at Stancliffe Hall, Darley Dale, 1890s. Standing, left to right: John Wilson, John Siddall, Henry Condliffe, George Smith, Bill Mason. Sitting: Henry Fearn, William Barker, Walter Wall. On the floor: Jack Allsopp, Henry Fielding.

Workers at Wildgoose's Quarry, Matlock Moor, *c.* 1914.

Workers at Stancliffe Quarry, Darley Dale, 1920s.

JAMES SMITH & SONS'

DARLEY DALE NURSERIES

The Founder of the Firm.

Near MATLOCK,
DERBYSHIRE.

The Late Proprietor.

The Present Proprietor.

James Smith & Sons, Darley Dale. This company ran a nursery of international reputation.

Darley Dale Nursery. This picture, from a brochure issued before the First World War, shows trees being packed for delivery to Kaiser Wilhelm of Germany.

The railway station, Cromford. The design of the Up platform (right) is attributed to G.H. Stokes, Sir Joseph Paxton's son-in-law.

A Midland Compound Manchester–St Pancras express, at the railway station, Cromford, pre-1923.

Railway cleaners at Rowsley, near Darley. During the Second World War women were employed as cleaners. Back row, left to right: Madge Wilmot, Rosie Mackley, Doris Holmes, Harriet Pinder, Pat Esplen, Doris Rudd, Daphne Evans, Mrs Evans, ? Boden. Front row: E. Parker, Annie Hiden, Doris Wager, O. Fean, Jack Hibbs (foreman), Edna Watken, Celia Middleton, Madge Elliot, E. Boam.

Station staff, Darley Dale. This photograph was taken in late LMS days before nationalization. Back row, left to right: George Gilbert, Frank Niven (ganger), Jack Boden, Herbert Ankers (lorry driver), Joe Taylor. Front row: Charlie Gratton, Brian Beresford, Arthur Rumble (stationmaster), Stan Aulty. The lady in the lorry is Zoë Bark.

The railway station, Matlock Bath, pre-1893. In keeping with the Alpine atmosphere of the Derwent gorge, the station was built in Swiss chalet style.

Station staff, Matlock, *c*. 1917. Those present include Mr Harry I'Anson (stationmaster) and local railway officials.

The railway station, Matlock. The original caption wrongly describes this as Matlock Bath station. At the time this picture was taken it would have been known as Matlock Bridge station.

A batch of recruits leaving for the Army in the First World War, the railway station, Darley Dale.

# Going to School

Stancliffe Hall, Darley Dale. This was the home of Sir Joseph Whitworth from 1871 until his death in 1887. The hall dates from Stuart times but has been renovated considerably over the years, in Sir Joseph's time by T. Roger Smith and E.M. Barry. After the death of Lady Whitworth in 1896 the hall was sold and became a school. It still continues as Stancliffe Hall Preparatory School for Boys.

The headmaster's study, Stancliffe School, Darley Dale, *c*. 1920s.

The library, Stancliffe School, Darley Dale, possibly 1920s.

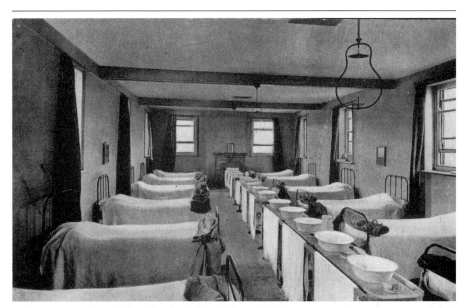

A dormitory at Stancliffe School, Darley Dale, *c.* 1920s.

A cricket match in progress on the cricket field, Stancliffe School, Darley Dale, possibly 1920s.

St Elphins School, Darley Dale. Formerly a hydro run by William Atkins, this became a school in 1904 when St Elphins moved from Warrington. Richmal Crompton, the author of the 'William' books, was a Classics mistress here for many years. The school continues to this day.

A classroom in the years between the wars, St Elphins School, Darley Dale.

A domestic science lesson between the wars, St Elphins School, Darley Dale.

An art lesson out of doors, St Elphins School, Darley Dale.

St Elphins School Hockey Team, Darley Dale, *c.* 1913.

Ernest Bailey Grammar School Girls' Hockey Team, Matlock, mid-1960s. Mr W. Horner (headmaster) is in the centre.

Infants at Churchtown School, Darley Dale, early this century.

Infants at Churchtown School, Darley Dale, *c.* 1915. Miss Maggie Siddall (teacher) is on the left and Mr Charles Scott Anthony (headmaster) is on the right.

Children at Churchtown School, Darley Dale, 1916. Those present include Mr Charles Scott Anthony (headmaster) and Miss Bagshaw (teacher).

Gardening at Cromford School. This subject formed a useful part of the curriculum at this time. The boys are sticking peas.

Gardening at Cromford School. The boys are trenching the ground in preparation for winter.

A lesson in winter pruning, Cromford School.

Gardening at Cromford School. The boys are learning how to plant from a demonstration by their teacher.

Indoor class at Cromford School. In the classroom more theoretical instruction is under way.

Cromford School outing. Some kind of nature walk or geological excursion appears to be in progress.

Bunting Cup Finalists, 1948.

Admissions at Matlock Council School, 1912. The School, opened in 1897, is now known as Matlock County School. The boys' collars look impractical and would not have stayed clean for long.

# The Social Scene

Hall Leas, Matlock. In 1899 the Hall Leas was bought by the Matlock Urban District Council as a place for public enjoyment. It has been well used ever since. There is provision for tennis and bowls, and there is a children's paddling pool. The bandstand (centre) has been used for concerts since the early part of this century.

Matlock Carnival, 1938. The carnival queen, Miss L. Knowles (centre; now Mrs Stuart Taylor), and attendants, Nina Kyte (left) and Laura Gratton (right), are present at the opening of Matlock Lido.

The audience at the opening ceremony of Matlock Carnival, 1938.

The wedding of Emily Evans and Cecil Goward, 1904.

The wedding of Stanley Fearn and Edith Mary Sergeant, St Helen's church, Darley Dale, 1913.

The Two Dales Wesleyan Sunday School, outside the Red House, Darley Dale. This appears to be a chapel walk. This picture was taken in the early part of this century.

The Matlock Motor Cycle and Light Car Club in a local quarry. The railway bridge is in the background. This picture was possibly taken in the late 1920s or early 1930s.

The Matlock Prize Choir, 1924. Choirs have always played a large part in Matlock life. Under the baton of Lubin Wildgoose many prizes were won. Here and below Wildgoose is pictured in the centre of the group.

The Matlock Prize Male Voice Choir, 1929.

The Matlock Primitive Methodist Contest Choir with their trophies, 1924. This choir was based at the Matlock Primitive Methodist chapel on Bank Road.

The Matlock Primitive Methodist Contest Choir, Matlock station, with a much older Lubin Wildgoose, returning in some triumph from a Festival of Britain contest, 1951. On Wildgoose's left is Ella Smith (then editor of the *Matlock Mercury*).

Matlock United Prize Band at Bob Davis's wedding, Poplar Hydro, 1895. The original Matlock Band was attached to the local Volunteers and wore their military uniform. After a period of abeyance the Matlock United Prize Band was re-formed in 1894. Back row, left to right: old Tant Holmes, Lot Fox, young Tant Holmes, Bob Davis, Tom Holmes, Ben Allwood, Alf Keeling. Middle row: Mick Frost, George A. Frost (?), Peter Rouse, Bill Holmes, Billy Crowter, ? Holmes. Front row: ? Holmes, ? Holmes, Andrew Swift.

Matlock Band on the bandstand in the Hall Leas, *c*. 1910. The small boy with the cornet (front row) was Fred Slater, who was to spend his life promoting brass bands in the Matlock area and who taught many people (including the author), without payment, to play a brass instrument.

Matlock Junior Band, early 1960s. Those present include Fred Slater (white jacket) and Murray Slater (back row, far left).

Matlock Band with contest trophies, late 1960s. Fred Slater is in the centre (front row).

Matlock Band playing in the street, early 1960s. Partly to provide Christmas cheer and partly to raise funds, the band has always toured the district at Christmas. Fred Slater is conducting.

Darley Dale Silver Band, Christmas 1936.

The Matlock Brotherhood Orchestra at the bandstand in the Hall Leas. Judging from the ladies' hats and shoes the date would appear to be in the late 1920s. Lubin Wildgoose is in the middle of the second row (with a double bass).

The High Tor Players in a production of Sheridan's *School for Scandal*, 1965. This is one of the oldest established amateur dramatic groups in the Matlock area and is still flourishing. Left to right: Cora Oliver, John Kent, Joyce Renner.

The High Tor Players in a production of *The Hollow* by Agatha Christie, 1953. Left to right: Anne Paulson, Fred Shaw, June Leggatt, Irene Morton, Eileen Redfern, John Martin, Eileen Stoneley, Alistair Story.

The High Tor Players, 1950s. These members off stage include Derek Redfern (back row, far right) and Eileen Redfern (front row, far right).

The Matlock Poultry Society Show, *c.* 1953. Mr B.C. Kidger is pictured with the Best Bird in Show, an Indian Game, bred by Mr R.D.G. Lane. This was the first annual show. The Matlock Poultry Society was founded in 1950.

Matlock Poultry Society annual dinner, 1954. Those present include Harry Fox (seated, far left), a well-known poultry expert, and Lewis Jackson (seated, far right), now a well-known builder and local councillor.

The Matlock Poultry Society Show, late 1950s. This group of members and prizewinners includes T. Kersey, T.F. Bower, Mrs C. Taylor, H. Slack, H. Petts, Mrs D. Bryer, W. Doxey, J. Marchant, Mrs A. Marchant and Miss D. Barton (now Mrs G. Coleman).

The Matlock Poultry Society Show at Whitworth Institute, early 1960s. Back row, left to right: J. Marchant, Mrs A. Marchant, D.A. Barton, O. Gratton, J. Jackson, H. Slack, Mrs Doxey, Mrs Mackfall, Mrs Slack. Middle row: G. Fielding, Mrs C. Taylor, W. Doxey. Front row: Miss D. Smith, Miss D. Barton (now Mrs G. Coleman), Trevor Slack.

The funeral of John William Wildgoose, 1923. Wildgoose was the head of the local building firm. His funeral took place at the Primitive Methodist Chapel on Bank Road, Matlock. The picture shows the junction between Smedley Street and Bank Road. Smedley's Hydro is on the left and the carriages are standing outside the chapel (right).

The procession at Charlie Dawson's funeral, May 1928. Mr Dawson, the manager of Stancliffe Quarry, Darley Dale, died in a car accident at Ashwood Dale, near Buxton. The procession is coming down Church Lane, Darley Dale, to St Helen's church.

Funeral cars and a hearse belonging to Joseph Allen & Sons, Crown Square, Matlock.

An Edwardian group in local transport by the Crown Hotel. There was always a demand for transport, whether to and from the station for patients from the hydros or purely for sightseeing.

A charabanc outside The Pavilion, Matlock Bath.

A ladies' outing from Bulwell, Nottinghamshire.

A rather overloaded coach standing by The Pavilion.

Two advertisements by William Furniss show the passage of time and the gradual take-over by the motor car.

For those as yet uncaptivated by speed, horse transport was still attractive, such as a four-in-hand charabanc (above) or a rather overloaded four-in-hand coach (below).

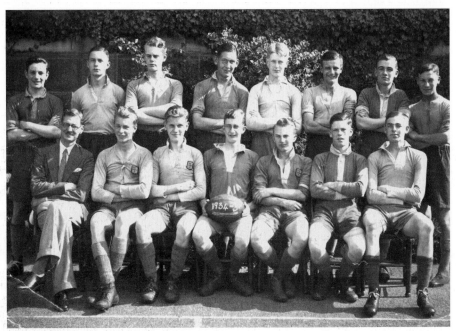

Ernest Bailey Grammar School Rugby Football Team, 1934. Those present include Ernest Paulson, now a local historian (back row, fourth from left).

Ernest Bailey Grammar School Rugby Football Team, 1949–50. Back row, left to right: J. Moreton, B. Wilson, C. Greatorex, R. Howes, R. Standen, B. Gale, M. Holmes, H. Daniel, B. Hobbs. Middle row: Mr W.E. Allen, J. Hancock, B. Gregory, J. Billingham (captain), W. Wass, R. Slack, L. Finney. Front: R. Duggins, O. Moore.

A rugby match between Ernest Bailey Grammar School and Lady Manners Grammar School, Bakewell, 16 March 1949. It was played at Cromford Meadows. The Ernest Bailey Grammar School boys (in dark shirts) won. Those present include: Colin Lomas, Bill Wass, Ron Slack, Stan Stone, Lew Finney, John Moreton, John Hancock, Henry Davies, Dick Standen, John Billingham (with arm in sling). The score was 5 points to 3.

The Darley Wanderers, a local Association Football team, sometime before the First World War.

The Matlock Cavendish Rovers, another local team, 1921–2.

Darley Dale Football Team, 1950.

Cromford Football Team, 1913–14.

Matlock Town Football Club, 1922–3. Back row, left to right: W. Johnson (secretary), ? Sowerly, ? Beaton, ? Lacy, ? Phillips, ? Mellors, ? Fancutt, ? Lamb, ? Lownham. Front row: ? Adams, ? Whittingham, ? Littlewood, ? Weldon, ? Barnett.

Matlock Junior Football Club, 1916.

Tennis players, Matlock, in the early part of this century.

Ernest Bailey Grammar School Girls' Tennis Team, 1948–9. Back row, left to right: -?-, Miss Lenthall, Shirley Croft. Front row: Jean Carson, Betty Gaythorpe, Liz Winder.

Darley Dale Cricket Team, 1895. This team were winners of the Derbyshire County Challenge Cup. Back row, left to right: T. Wright (secretary), F. Evans, B.C. Gregory (captain), A.H. Smith (vice-captain), J. Siddall, W.M. Holmes. Middle row (leaning on columns): Ben Gregory, R.J. Wright. Front row: J. Gregory (umpire), C. Pashley, R.B. Wright, H. Gregory, J.J. Willgoose, W. Gregory.

Matlock Bath Ladies' Cricket Team, possibly 1930s.

Cromford Scouts. The Scout movement began after the publication of Baden-Powell's *Scouting for Boys* in 1908, but this postcard is difficult to date.

'Local Patriots, 1914'. This caption accompanied this picture of the Matlock Signallers in the local paper, though it is not clear what their purpose was. Left to right: C. Daniels, R.S. Baumber, S.W. Bailey, G. Cocking, E.D. Edwards (instructor), J.J. Shaw, E. Holmes.

Mrs Sanderson and her children at
Tansley, between 1910 and 1915.

Tom Marsh and his wife at Tansley,
between 1910 and 1915.

# MATLOCK HOUSE HYDROPATHIC ESTABLISHMENT

AND

## RESIDENCE FOR VISITORS,

# MATLOCK BRIDGE, DERBYSHIRE.

Physician: Dr. W. MOXON, L.R.C.P. Edin., M.R.C. Eng

FOR TERMS, ADDRESS MANAGER.

---

## Stevenson's Hydropathic Establishment & Boarding House

### BELLE VUE, MATLOCK BANK, DERBYSHIRE.

### ESTABLISHED 1860.

The above Establishment is about **a quarter of a mile from Matlock Bridge Station, on the Midland Railway,** and is well situated, commanding views of the most beautiful scenery in England. It is sheltered from the North and East Winds, and well supplied with pure soft water from the sandstone rocks.

The system of Hydropathy practised is precisely the same as that used by the late John Smedley, viz,: The **Mild Water Treatment,** the baths being regulated to suit the condition of each patient.

**PROSPECTUS, TERMS, &c., POST FREE ON APPLICATION.**

A typical advertisement for a hydropathic establishment.

Charles White, MP from 1863 to 1923. Standing as Liberal candidate in 1918, Charles defeated Lord Kerry and won the seat for the Liberals for the first time since the constituency was set up in 1885. Tragically he died during the 1923 election campaign.

Charles White (junior) (1891–1956). Charles stood as Independent Labour candidate in 1944 and again defeated the Conservative candidate, the Marquis of Hartington. He held the West Derbyshire seat for Labour until 1950. He was the leading promoter of the scheme to move the county council headquarters from Derby to Smedley's Hydro.

# Acknowledgements

Producing a book of this kind depends very much on the generosity and help of local people. There are many who have trusted me with their treasured photographs and therefore numerous people whom I must thank. Foremost among these are Glyn Waite and Ken Smith, who have supplied me with pictures, and without whose help the book would not have been possible; also Robert Lake, formerly of Tansley, whose excellent pictures have enabled me to cover Tansley to a greater degree than I had thought possible.

My sincere thanks also go to the following, who gave me advice and loaned their photographs:

Norman Ash • John Billingham • the staff of the County Record Office, Matlock
Andrew Derbyshire • Mr W. Ellis • Sam Fay • Geoff Fearn
Derek Goodall of M. Wright & Sons • Mr N. Goward of W. Evans & Son
Mrs Hodgson of St Elphin's School • Mrs Gloria Hollingworth
David Hool • John Kersey • Terry Kilburn • Mrs Rebecca Kirby
Lawrence Knighton • Derek Lane • the staff of the Local Studies Library
Ernest Paulson • Mrs Joyce Renner • Mrs E. Revell
Mr R.W.M. Shaw of the Army Intelligence Corps Museum • Murray Slater
Ron Slack • Herbert Taylor • Harold Wardman • Angus Watson • Ron White
Dr Lyn Willies and the Lyn Willies Collection, including those from Ron Slack,
E. Fisher, William Else, Harry Parker and the Stone Collection.

Finally, thanks as always to Gwyneth, my wife, for both her encouragement and her powers of organization.

Derbyshire Library Service maintains a large collection of photographic material relating to the county which is held in the Local Studies Libraries at Derby and the Library Headquarters at Matlock. If you have any old photographs of the county which you would be prepared to donate or to lend for copying by the Library Service your local library would be pleased to see them.